Insel

INSEL

J. Michael Yates

The Queen Charlotte Islands
Meditations

Penumbra Press, 1983

Published by PENUMBRA PRESS , P.O. Box 340, Moonbeam,
Ontario, Canada POL 1VO, with financial assistance from
The Canada Council and The Ontario Arts Council.

ISBN 0 920806 58 9

for Colonel Joel H. Yates who, from wise distance, has watched my voyages with warmth, sagacity, and immense dread.

There, then, he sat, holding up that imbecile candle in the heart of that almight forlornness. There, then, he sat, the sign and symbol of a man without faith, hopelessly holding up hope in the midst of despair. *Moby Dick*

This winter in which you find me is not your winter.

Because things much more dangerous than death remain
unreined by names, they cannot, like island horses, be broken.
Nor shot to part them from their pain.

When the colourless hand of fog closes over the coast, it is not
death, but it is not living.
Preferring to bide its opposite, things bide time instead.
Time to fangle, time to become a beach between at least two
more and more unequal distances.
There are choices: Become a larger fisherman. Or a
fisherman smaller. The boats lengthen or grow shorter. And
fewer. Always fewer.
Begin fishing in deep winter. Go landless, navigate your
vessel away from all harbours, have a go at the high ocean
rollers.
After an unknown number breaks over the bow, expect the
ice to begin and win and win until everything above water-line
overbalances like a hydrocephalic child.

At the capsize comes an easing of decision: when the hands blue and loosen, when the jagged air is to no further point, when none cries out to no one in fear any longer, and none pauses to warn, and the northern night settles down in its blackness to a coast of a few smug lighthouses and a few dimly interrogative horns.

I can see more than one snowpeak from this beach. Alaska. On a lucid day.

Something of me, on the move always, busy in more than one time in more than one place.

Sound of a seaplane approaching from somewhere above the cover.

Footsteps of a stone-age tribe of shellfish-eaters coming toward me in bad darkness and in bad light going away.

And no word will speak exactly one stone subtracted from all possible beach.

You are forward. I am aft. Control of outboard engine is mine. You've brought your thirty-ought-six fishing to blow hell out of dog-sharks that might nuisance our lines. In the service of commercial fishermen, you will kill; in memory, possibly, of drowning sailors clinging to rocks; for the future of small children wading the shallows of the saltchuck almost anywhere.

Tide falling, and over your right shoulder, on my left, I notice the rock full of sea-lions and seals that foul and rob the nets of commercial fishermen, screw up the gill-netting in the middle of a perfect run, and commit other high marine crimes, and I nose us toward them keeping your face toward me, knowing that any second the herd will decide that we are we and judder back down the rock-side into the water and dive, goddammit, dive, and don't come up for air until you're miles from here.

Their fact comes and goes away without your knowledge and saltspray chewing all the pretty off your gun. You sip your beer and squint at the rod-tips as we troll.

I don't love God's creatures nor even God. No. And, yes, I had to come all this distance and partly become you over all these years to learn I loathe a part of your imbecile, Canadian, northbilly soul.

At the sandy graveside, looming thunderheads of words close away the light.

Thus the sea breathes in, easily, one more long and negligible history.

Before the land writes one man, it blots a thousand thousand.

Child, may you never notice that seabirds, electrons, and galaxies are also only words.

Pulse unsteady at the speed of dark.
  Do not attempt to catch falling objects. Especially debris of
failing light.
  When the full ovoid moon of my demon squints over the
horizon of reason,
    When I have come north as far as I can come,
    There remains only, without watch, without compass,
entrance into the calling wild.
    Loosing of the mind to hunt the mind amid the shadowy
talus of lightscape.

Don't let them do it under cover of darkness.
  They will do it in any case, but don't let them, dammit, do
it in the dark.
  To defy gods, to glory them, and in spite of us, they will
do it.
  But let us pact and cause them to do what they do in our
light,
  That one or two might notice and recall the price of nothing
at all.

This winter in which you find me is not my winter.
  It doesn't fit. And neither can be altered.
  Take it away.

What lingers here still hushes and gives on the wind:
  Intimation of another time when these same cedars whittled
grand men into frightened little boys.
  How to have known these silences independent of my noise.

At sudden places, through this tree-tunneled way toward Rose
Spit and the cease of land, a plank road—hand-fitted,
ancient—insists through the sand like a battle won in a war
long, long ago, lost.

Now and then the citizen wins a battle. Reluctantly. Humbly.
But the madman of me loves the whole war.

No, not innocence, I have not come north again to recover an
innocence of which I slaved to be rid. It is my sacred
worthlessness I wish to exhume.

Island north is new and not new to me. What is new, perhaps, lives only in the view, vision, sight, standing calf-high in cougar-coloured grass from a sea-cliff hill between Skidegate and Tlell, through wind sharp as a d-adze, toward Cormorant Rock. The dark basalt alive with things which cock and fire their necks of s-shape spring and open and close their in and out of water wings.

Their purpose—these blots of rock, these bent animals, this carver's wind—is not clear. Sometimes it has to be enough. To be. Merely. To be. Here. Squirt by squirt of the heart.

Time and tide, exhaling here, now, after the long breathing-in of being young. Here on the subsiding side of both time and tide, among the clear pools full of things waiting for water to return, the steel-coloured sea-blade carving far out and almost out of sight, falling and falling and almost at low-slack. Time now to say inside it is almost good to know for a certainty with the blood: I can die. With luck, the tide of knowing won't rise to the brain for a little while longer. And inhale. And remember: there was a woman I once cared for most when she most smelled of northern low tide.

What enters the amber eye of the cormorant never reaches an
organ which thinks or tries to think or cares that a dark figure
across the blowing water atop a seahill stands there trying to
think about not thinking, carefully not voicing a postulate such
as: I don't think, therefore I am not. This is a possibility which,
possibly, even I could care about.

That you cannot disprove my certainty that I am not sane, does
not, therefore, prove my sanity.
   That I am still at large among you neither polishes nor flaws
your expert vanity.

Those who come to these islands come in fright, come from
frightening places to here which, frightening as it is, seems less
frightening, for a little while, than every other frightening place.

Like geese and teal and widgeon and certain other animals of
water and air, certain of us pause from flight here, uncertainly,
to eat and drink whatever there is, to fuck what is now and then
willing, or doesn't, momentarily, care—then, again, fly.

Evidence of my having been somewhere sometimes takes on the appearance of life. In times of luck, news arrives several stops behind me.

Flight was never a way of life. Neither was life in the nesting.

I don't remember the rest, but her letter thus came to the end of itself: *My body, however pretty, is disposable; not so, the rest. I don't care who I fuck so long as who I fuck doesn't.*

Flight is the solitary goose-cry in the night of being frightened of all but one thing.

Flight was always and never the voice of being frightened of everything.

Getting elsewhere is one way of not staying and, with luck, not saying: I can't stay here anymore and there's no understanding to it; with luck, not lying: I'll see you, this place, again, later, again, it's been good, I'm only leaving for a sojourn, I won't be long, I'll call, I'll write, the time will pass, yes, yes, very quickly; not, with luck, saying to myself: thus it begins again, the flow which folds me in and drowns on toward the lightless sea-floor at the end of all further places to go.

Let motion be the real estate I own. Let me sign in the script of time on the dotted line of the deed.

Out of flight, I try and again try to coax a way of life.
Goddamn the part of the heart opposed to this.
Of escape I make a place to live. Almost. Not quite. I am full of this certainty: surely not all of escape has been staked, subdivided, occupied.

Accidentally, I am blowing out the lantern of what I know with
the black breath of what I cannot possibly.

Love of edge. Have lived it. Always I have lived toward love of
edge, of the gleaming, of the treasured blade of nothing,
　　Its voyage through sapwood toward the core, the fleet wedge
of used beauty to be driven between the dead ends of duty,
　　Ending, after the back-cut, in spent gaze which fixes on the
fall: doors of gravity opening, gravity rising to claim. Gravity,
receiving.

...I'm serious about the whales　*Jack Gilbert*

Fluke. Seamark for a vanishing point: thus, then, these flukes
fan, undreamable, sheening this evening without evening
breeze.
　　Somewhat sunset, somewhat silhouette, rooted somewhere
unreasonable beneath the salt skin of sea; bole, twin mammoth
fronds; one sense invents the scent of prehistoric flora.
　　This evening empty of evening breeze, the living kingdoms
merge: half an animal mirages half a tree.

Lake surrounded by land surrounded by sea.

Archaic water. Colour of peat whiskey. So used, the fabric of surface begins wearing through.

So many things, so much like lives, enter their beauty only while dying. Or ill. Or supposing.

The mind swings like the needle of a compass between sentences of treatment and sentences of punishment.

The hand upon the power-saw is undeterred. The alder and fireweed springing back to reclaim what belongs to a wilderness are undeterred.

Everything is winning.

And none.

North is the heaviest judgement of a wilderness upon a mind. Prison is the heaviest judgement on the mind by what a wilderness is not.

Unless the mind consents, whereupon the sense of sentence rearranges itself, and what or who judges vanishes into ice-fog or into white-out or into mist.

At a certain extreme of extremity, all sentences, formal and informal, interchange.

The case does not rest.

In this geography of north the language of north is understood by almost all. And spoken by almost none.

Here, it is possible to grow so preoccupied with the detail of the environment that one forgets it is here to live in.

Here, it is possible to grow so preoccupied with insulating one's life against the threat of the environment that he does not live within it.

Far, deep, away in the south of my time alive, I condense the many into one redwing blackbird whose stray voice
Deeper and deeper seeps through the high, fuzzing cattails of my fisheryouth:
Old now, silent now, the creature is captive still inside the collapsing boyhood of dream.
Collapsing.
That fine capture of golden animal light.

I have failed to cure my compass of north and the needle no longer homes there in any way known to me.

Like houses of cards, tall towers of importances collapse and reorganize themselves here.

How one arrives here has little to do with how mainland minds move from one place to another place.

What can be taken for granted—these tones of uncertainty—are not what one takes for granted in the place called 'outside'.

The ways to die are extraordinary by terms of ordinary lives.

So it is with insular north and with prison. In these places, even the unusual must be approached unusually. For survival, the routine must come to seem extraordinary. Commonplace: the extreme.

I have come to know—the complicated way—sanctuary in surroundings of terror. That a world through the wrong end of the telescope is also a world. That I prefer not to die among the hordes dying of safety.

Certain things can persist only in the languages of what they are not.

Certain things are as they are, like powerlines: held definite only by their bonds, with or without consent.

A north.

A prison.

Mere ideas, therefore not dangerous until expressed. And for a few, not dangerous even then.

Mere forms which feed on the energy of fantasy; therefore delicate and they starve to death easily.

Two of numberless steamy windows opening on a nameless metaphor.

He was one who had come to love dark. He surmised so. And that he truly allowed his process through the long, soft gut of darkness, the singular peristalsis of aurora, all senses circulating close, like the blood of cold.

His life had become a refinement of the art of remaining merely metabolic, and when death came to him again and again, he didn't give a damn whether to woof or bite.

When lowest temperature arrived and kicked the struts out from under what it is that holds refuse aloft in the sky of the skull, he could see clean—almost—through to the timeward border of infinity.

They said he was poet laureate of Alaska.

He said it was embarrassing.

He made his living as a Lutheran minister and the man couldn't decide which was worse—the preacher as shadow of the poet, or the reverse.

He ransacked north looking for a durable thread on which to string all of his days and failed and wrote a book called *God Has Been Northward Always* anyway. Then one entitled *Green Peter*, full of northy myth and tongues. 'English,' his wide, arctic owl face opened, 'was never a language of the north. Nor French. It is blasphemy, their jabbering Arabic up here—at more than sixty below.' Languages of the north, he was sure, are carved word by word in the north by the north. And those who speak them are ventriloquized by the universal northward soul.

It then occurred to him to convert from *Prädiger* to bush university teacher and did and his books didn't slip into place on those shelves with notable ease.

When he taught, you learned his huge hands, knuckles were strung together like molecules on a model of a chemical compound.

He had studied with Roethke, who was , of course, crazy; but, on the other hand, neither was he. And there the comparison doesn't end. He didn't play tennis and savage his knees on clay courts (there are other courts of clay), his knees were okay; nor did he play ping pong at all (let alone as if life were on the line with each deuce). He didn't wish to be life's fool—never mind how the suspicions nipped him—nor die foolishly, diving into a rich man's chilly swimming pool on a hot northwestern day. He was big and bearish like Roethke and so taught and did his utmost to go crazy in a university and didn't and perhaps inspired none to deathless poetry.

He died of something unpoetic and likely not sacred in the least.

One hand of his belonged to something usual and the other to something unique.

The northern air his hands fondled and flayed lives a little still in a few churches and classrooms and sometimes nearly speaks.

North, deep north. Poseidon, landlord of water, skulks the sands of island coast—sulking. Seeming fearful. Strangely despairing of his seas.

An oilslick translates itself from the surf to the sand beneath his feet. This spotted serpent of beach coils ninety miles without intrusion of right-of-way.

The data of north is no longer flowered.

Unlike its bewildered history.

Far into night sight, when the skunk-cabbage coloured frogs and black-button crickets fall silent, listening toward a sound unknown to them and coming their way, I can dream the genocidal yellow cedar back on their high side-hills speaking of form with trees very much alive still in my library downstairs. Alive inside each surgically violated page.

Only in angry rapture, might a god carve this voluptuous killer terrain.

The ones here whose nicknames I learn, the ones who die almost daily of *wilderchine*, of the place where bush and mechanical behemoth no longer exist independent of one another: these who die here take less and less of me away with them to their uncharted archipelago of darkness, but leave this increasing reef which is visible only at minus tide of the memory.

In memory of Albert Edenshaw, head chief of _____
Born 1822, Died 189___
A member of St. John's Church
A staunch friend to the White Man
He heroically saved the life of Capt. Rooney
and his crew of the Sch. Susan Sturges
attacked by Indians, Sept. 26, 1852,
for which he is held in grateful remembrance.

In memory of Capt. Matthew Rooney of Sch. Susan Sturges. Born and died. Piloted from Skidegate to North Island by Al Edenshaw, wife, and son around Rose Spit. Enroute, traded with and was tricked and boarded by Old Chief Weah, lost command, boat plundered. One of the dumbest Yanks ever to sell more ass than he could afford to buy back. Edenshaw salvaged the carcass of his memory for blankets.

In memory of Old Chief Weah, not tame Henry, born and died Haida time, Haida space. Died with a savage smile on his face. Placed atop burial poles, stank on the wind among the trees, high off the ground for the spirit to move at ease in honest pursuit of power, property, sex and gaud. In death, no staunch friend to the honoured historical fraud.

It is not that island time means more dimly than all other time.

It is that the form and energy of this island Yakoun River resemble the breath and depth of no other river.

Because of Yakoun time, nothing is landlocked. There are no non-sea-run fish. No non-sea-run dreams. All things living, eventually, voyage toward the sea. Nothing is landlocked here. Except, possibly, a man consenting. Possibly a man like me.

Time here frequently suspends. Or slows toward cease, as all sound seems to cease when, dim and deep in the interior spell, the drumming of a single grouse erases the huge boom of a falling seven-hundred-year-old spruce.

Deeper than sapwood, I could become something almost authentic among these numberless colours of green. Except for the No in me that remains inaccessible, high on a steep side-hill somewhere.

Better this decided distance; better to smoke a cigarette in order to keep something between island and me; better to say one word aloud, alone; better to leave one boot-print in the wet memory of volcano.

No.

I could undress, conceal myself, and, like all else here, transpire. Breathe. Simply breathe.

Today, one or more will say: The view is beautiful, simply beautiful.

And that's right. And that's all. Today is merely beautiful. A drunk for the senses and offense to imagination.

Distance is not without mercy.

No.

Some will suppose it fear. Still: No.

Never, perfectly, will this moment in this place exit me.

And there is no way for me quite in.

As the wharves zipper together land and water, hold on. Hold it together. For the quick, forever is not long.

Dad? Yes. *Can you come to this island where I am?* I hope so.
Soon? I'll try. *The day after today?* Soon. *It's very dark where I
am, you know?* I think I can remember. *Can you come here and
help with the dark?* I think.... *Can you?...come?...help?* I
will. *What can you do?* I'll think of something. *When?* Before
the pontoons touch the beach right in front of where you are.
Dad? Yes. *Well, it's dark right now where I am, you know?* I'll
think of something. *But couldn't you think right now? Instead?*

Light-years between me and my writing place, two rooms
away. I haven't the fare to travel there and wouldn't know
where to pay.

I'm well. I exercise. I'm well. Well. I prowl reaches of beach
exceeding stamina and sight. For more than a year, no alcohol
nor tobacco have entered me. Logging has trimmed my body as
something else should have done my mind.

Voice skewers the reverie, that of a student explaining to my
colleague that she and others are setting forth to free the people.
His reply: Christ, life is tough enough without having to cope
with being freed.

Teaching was a mainland; I am an island now. Freed.

I speak. I can hear my speaking in the distance.

I travel to the kitchen for a glass of water I didn't know I needed. I moor at the dining-room window and vanish through the glass into the fuming blue of Masset Inlet pressed against its sky: young geese, mallards, widgeon, and teal from the wide wetlands at the rivermouth arabesque in formation above the water like dancing oriental fans.

When I nose about in the mossy yard, neighbours and passers nod kindly and never eye me with more than expected suspicion of one maimed by overeducation and an obsession that joins no union and does not win ostensible bread.

It has not rained excessively: black flies and noseeums have come and all but gone; money is sufficient; the killing of deer and fish for the table does not beard my conscience; refusal to shoot sea-lion, eagles, and bear provides no holiness; I'm logged with the quiet I journied here to acquire; I am warm, I am dry; by a woman who does not intrude, I am well cared for, perhaps unoppressively loved; nothing is missing; I am without desire for any previous or future elsewhere; the continent has not yet filed itself as 'outside'; I am far enough windward of forty; no hatred comes to mind; light has not yet begun to trick the aspect of my world as it later will.

Later, things and I will not occur exactly as we seem. Later, possibilities like barber-shops, pharmacies, and mainlands will slip smoothly out of memory like coins from a pocket worn through. Later the beast of existence will try to shake me from its hide and the other side of time will take on more and more lure; I will inch toward it on bad footing.

Later.

And again.

Just now, I am well. The galaxy in my skull whirs with coloured stars of untruth to compose for voice and page.

Something insists that to oil a pair of caulk boots with care, hands and leather almost one, is a finer priority than words.

I ignore and ignore my own maxim that all time to write is stolen time.

The hunter is his own ultimate quarry to outwit—the line trots forward to join others, finds nothing waiting for its arrival, then falls away in long shadows like Pacific sunset.

I'm well. Dangerously well. I can fall from the broad, safe back of this. No so perfectly counterweighs Yes.

Around the continent where most of me persist, these islands perforate the sea like stars which flaw the continuous tone of dark: an otherwise perfect routine of eternity.

Almost no one prefers to dwell on an island indefinitely.

One island is smaller than one continent and growing smaller tide by tide.

Of those who go to islands for short stays then return to conceal where they have been behind the faces of mainland ways, it is difficult to speak.

Legend has it that every island is the summit of a sunken mountain.

The many—only those who pause to notice islands—suppose islands notes toward a mainland never concluded.

An island can be infinite only to a few among the few.

An early part of me ferries freely from mainland to island; then more and more often it remains and remains until it is possibly too late.

Less and less answers when fume of the human burning bids what is left come to mainland horn.

What crosses to an island and overstays: its name and relics are kept by a few for an instant. The life which once belonged to the evidence will not recur.

Of those who somehow lose their ways to both island and mainland, there should be something to say.

There ought to be something for the ones who, for no easy reason, weary under only part-way back. When the vessel has finally done with its long, awkward sinking, sometimes a stream of bubbles fumbles up. This becomes a curiosity. Until it becomes too familiar to be noticed any more.

Few such sea-marks appear these days. And far fewer stop and point and exclaim that here or over there, north of those sea-cliffs bronze in strong stormlight, exactly there: authentic craft once sailed.

Inside the dark body of the real, what I point to only resembles what I think it is, what you accept it as, what we hang a word on, then a diminutive; then the invocation with forced fearlessness, lion-tamer's familiarity.

There are the words.

There are the things.

There I am working both sides of the street, trying to bang a life out of confusing the two.

The words were never the things. Things had to be before words. My body was before its noun. Nouns tend to lie down together: with luck, my noun with your noun through the good service of a hardy verb.

There is an office of time which links unnamable, named things.

Reason is certain that things must have been before syllables to signify in their stead. The Dawson Caribou before its moniker, then the volumes of *extinct* to fill the places of its insular absence.

Something not reason is not at all certain. Something somewhat God.

Words in their own lives insist on being things. And things are never quite things until they wear names. This leads the mind again circular into the dark body of suspicion. A word might, at least once, antecede a thing, might turn flesh, turn light, and enter a comprehensive body of the dark.

Announce the environment has been settled: the dam will go up on schedule. With a hole in the centre to allow the river to run through.

What confirms life can kill. And will.

He loved wine.

No wine entered him.

It was necessary to remain steadily ready for the gods of darkness to exceed their drunken shiftlessness and arrive.

He died not drunk but hungry. Without knowing whether he had ever been ready. Without knowing whether his summons had ever been served.

Much scotch has gone into me. Now none.

The gods show and no-show as it pleases them.

I awaken to the sound of a pen gouging a page. No memory of entrance into the drunk.

Hours and months pass for which — other than this — I have no account at all.

Like a big motorcycle with a fine engine clenched in a terrible frame, wobbling and washing through a turn, almost in the hands of random: like this, the gillnetter writhes through the narrow entrance-way, juddering toward the refuge of a cove the map insists exists and promises depth enough and one tiny island we can duck behind and ride easy in the lee.

All day we have surfed and plowed the great rollers up from the ocean floor on the west side of the islands, no land-mass to interrupt imagination between here and Japan.

It is good, almost magnificent, to go, to have been far out and away from all landmarks familiar, out of sight of land, among gulls which know nothing, away from the ravens full of knowledge of everything.

A life can change because of having been out far.

Then the light hunts lower, like a kingfisher over a school of grilse, soon to drop. Then the turning back for a place to night. The russet-coloured face-work of the big island appears and jags the easy curve of horizon. Close watch of the sonar. One peers casually over the gunwale, then over the bow, as the door to the cove opens too quickly.

Return should be a different thing.

Depth is not exactly right. The map is evasive on the subject of currents. Stone silent in the matter of wind. Wind claws the steep stone above with the frenzy of a demon caged. Wind fills and burns the ears. Almost as if I could spread my arms wide and touch rock on either side. Pike-poles at the ready...one might horse position against sea-force...none tries....The screw reverses, raging and scrambling and losing against the tidal flex and I suck my lungs full of maniacal wind and say aloud, unheard: *This is as good as a place as any.*

This passage has the feel of evil but without its personal attention.

The water will batter the entrance with boat and bones splintered, or without them. In this merge of matter and energy RIGHT NOW, this is no significant point. A narrows somewhere wild inside me fills with the forces of all my goings-away and comings-back and the teeth of land are bared like a family dog astoundingly gone berserk and turned. The high sea was frightening in its wideness but more friendly.

At the bark of an order, I jam a pole against an outcrop close and lean my life into the scream of the desperate diesel. The ass-end comes to but too far around and the helm again spins and I am back in Ohio on a Norton Atlas, deep into a tightening-radius turn whose camber changes midway for the worse, it is night or evening enough to be called night, like now, the centre-stand touches and the jingggg climbs my spine, I grab more angle and the left peg touches down, the spark-shower looks like the Fourth of July to the guy coming into the slot behind me, *You don't stuff it into an interesting turn wondering whether you should have done this, you negotiate the sonofabitch, Yates, negotiate*, and I am drafting an agreement with gravity and centrifugal force, the outside sole of my boot takes a rub and I can feel the grin spreading from lips to shoulder-blades, if I roll off the power now I'll be all over this old-mountain landscape, the force which got me into this is holding me here on this edge alive, alive on this strange high ridge between absolute panic and absolute grace, one last feather to the front brake for trim, the snakey curve uncoils, I kick down a gear and roll it on hard toward red-line, a rooster-tail of adrenalin rising the air behind me.

Inexplicably, with a last twitch of torque and wheel and feel of way between forces, the hull—almost on its own—clears, breaks free of the chop, and we enter the smooth, still lee of the rock which almost sank us, and enter the safety which, in excess, can kill more quietly and efficiently than risk.

I have been a war.

When I'm over, who will there be to despair over the evidence, to bury the fallen moss-chandeliers which come to resemble parts of things human which come to resemble, sometimes, something more.

Who to burn the treaties.

Who to reconstruct the space and cleanse it.

And who, cool and healing, to overweave my fire-perforations of the silence?

Footing once firm on the wharf gives the quick twitch and sag of danger.

Something has to be done about something from time to time to time.

My good madness strays. My good madness malingers among things cast up by suck of moon and things cast down by me not soon enough.

In the sea-noon light, a strut falls away, beneath a wharf built to weather and stay put beyond all face-lifts of land and all quick decisions of evil-mooded sea.

An old dog, crazed by being both dog and old, looses its life upon the sand, scattering the scatter of time and water, until it finds and rolls tirelessly in the high carcass of bits unfit for touch by even the farthest finger-tips of mind.

Nothing is behind it all.

I spy it sometimes peering around the corner of my eye as I bend down to reach for an urgent shape of drift or draw back to send a stone back into the breakers, giving it — for an instant — a life unlike all other stones.

Perhaps, around the next headland, or the next, I'll turn and — for an instant — face nothing, no longer hedging just beyond the rim of a motorcycle mirror nor dodging among sun-glitzed motes of dust in a room at the line between dusk and deep afternoon, but face nothing square-on for the first time. Or first, seemingly.

Around the next headland: perhaps just beyond a hollow drift-log I'll rig a photograph of myself inside (to prove to me I was both there and then), perhaps near the skeleton of mahogany decking of a ship killed there more than fifty years ago, still sinking through beach, bow accusing the sky still, like Laocoon.

Then, around the next headland, I'll go on. And forget for all purposes of words exactly what I've seen. And know, as uselessly as before, exactly what I've known.

Dear Outside:

No, please do not come here. Something has happened. Things as they were between me and what is not me are not as they are.

35

March, Yellow Point: a less populous place on a more civilized island. I am hiding here from my other island.

Dear Mainland:

Today is the first high sun of the cold solstice. Heavily sweatered, stiff as the lawn-chair I fill, I note that shapes of the tame surf here restate themselves in stone. Splayed before me and beneath high, chilly light, these horizontal pillars of basalt tongueing the hem of low tide could be abstracts by Giacometti. If Giacometti could be said to do abstracts. And if his tools included bubbles in magma and time sunken far into the mind of sea.

Yellow Point is the moniker for this watering place for cringers. I've heard 'Pointe Jaune' and 'Gelber Punkt' in the past while. While passes as time's name when the usual notations do not apply. Yellow Point: the designation is ill at ease in every language—like the name of a disease one whispers for fear it might hear and presume itself summoned.

I'd rather say I've gone for R. & R. to the Yukon, Kluane Lake, Destruction Bay.

Yellow gives the whole of the damn spectrum a bad name. Think of death in Lorca and Lorca in it in '36, in my mind the man died in yellow light, that yellow of Picasso's 'Guernica', the death yellow in his own *Bodas de Sangre*. Yellow was the last colour Borges saw before the shutter of his sight slammed.

Yellow Point: a couple of words for a couple of hundred
beach-front acres on an island voyaging through the magma
and bubbles of time and space. Good handle for whatever it is
that kills you or has been killing you from the beginning,
whenever it was or was not. To pursue the point would be to
say something for or against D.N.A., then work forward or
downward to the guy up the way a hundred yards in a beach
cabin alone with his case of rye. His manner stinks of medico,
specialist, big loot. Classic alcoholico taking the geographic
cure. El Borraco by eight at night. Me, I'm fine, useless as the
tits on the 'Marine Venus', but righteously, virtuously dry.
Me, I'm fine (just wanted to see if I could write it out again.).
Just fine.

Long, long is the tradition that a sickness be taken to a place,
a place different from the place of its beginning, if that place is
known. They bring their sicknesses to this place from all over
the world and speak of them, when at all, in languages not
understood by the maladies they bring. In this way, it reminds
me—not to excess—of my old *Kurstadt*, Wiesbaden. A haunt
beloved by Dostoievski; he gambled heavily there, at the
Kurhaus and on the page, the poor-house never distant from his
seizures, his excesses, his rage. My good growing up was there,
during the occupation and after. They came even then for the
cure, whatever it was, stepped around the small mounds of
piled paving stones and peered through unusual holes in
bombed gothic walls. Just coming to look was possibly part of
the cure. A cure-town is a cure-town; you can't bomb and strafe
away a cure.

Anything is a cure, or can become one, and any cure can invent a sickness to fit.

Syphillis, epilepsy, and consumption: by tradition, only these three ways to die find favour in the literary eye. And I don't qualify. They don't make diseases as they did in the old days. Or cures are better than ever.

In any case, Yellow Point is no Berghof; a Hans Castorp wouldn't hack it here two days, let alone seven years.

Most of the diseases transported here are vague, nameless, non-specific as a socked-in island afternoon, and most have been socked-in.

What ails me has a name, many names. It is more certain, more fixed to my substance than the high resolution of my shadow at two P.M. in the first high sun of the cold solstice. To name a complaint is not necessarily to quell it.

I am where will and lack of it equalize. At a yellow point, you might say. Only hesitant air blowing, only this squinty sunshine, and everything getting over-with at roughly 4500 heart-spasms an hour. Fear of not moving keeps me moving. I must move now, now, now, move on.

There is a cure for me. There is a cure for magma. It is called rock.

The craft threads through islands without tree, free of human evidence, but swarmed by white birds.

There are birds of other colours. One sees the white.

The birds see three-hundred-sixty degrees, and possibly degrees without assigned numbers.

There is a refuge in nakedness and exposure to terrible weather.

A craft alone in strange water goes insular and passes into danger.

An island in motion appears on no map.

Et êtes-vous écrivain?

Je suis poète.

Et avez-vous des livres?

Funny thing, I happen to have a couple with me.

She smiles beyond her best Air Canada smile and to the far walls of the bar, to the city limits of Montreal, to the Quebec-Ontario border, I can hear the waist-elastic of her knickers snap.

My true photographer keeps a naked lens between his eye and other eyes.

While the passing world averts nervously, he watches imperfectly.

All wars end.

Wars begin nowhere exactly but wars end in beginnings like: After the war, I had to get away, it was necessary, it was necessary to come north as far as I could go, and so....

And so on.

Look at this map. One-hundred-fifty-four islands. The pattern looks like a well-placed land-mine detonating, looks like a grenade exploding—you know what they call them now? *anti-personnel devices*, heh, *fragmentation weapons*, Christ, a man ought to kill a man with something whose name sounds like what it does, like Howitzer; I met this kid a while back who told me he *fragged* his own second looie—this looks like someone nuked the Pacific for being the wrong green on the right day…this map.

And so on.

All wars end. Except for the monuments and the monumental days and the speeches and the memorial archives in the head and the silences that end with: Before the war…during the war…after the war I came to these islands, come look at the map.

I needed, really needed to come as far north as I could go.

Everything has a beginning, a during, and an end. And that's not the end of it: everything has a before.

Before the war, I had hope, I had a lot of hope. My wife—who lost seven years of skirmishes and battles with cancer, and, finally, the war—used to say of me that before the war, all I wanted was a war, and maybe it was so….

And so here I am. And there I was. Missed one war but not the next. In 1949, I was the marine on the poster pointing at you saying Uncle Sam Wants You. And so…oh, fuck, I was beautiful, young, trim, six-feet-four and the youngest top sargeant in the Corps.

I knew the words to every World War II song and missed being in all the good places to sing them. But my time was coming. I never lost hope, no...I was drunk with hope. We never heard of north in California (and that almost sounds like a Beach Boys song) but we heard and loved the sound of marching (grew up next door to Camp Pendleton and woke up every morning to sound of close-order drill) and loved the look of beautiful uniforms...no, never heard of north, much less thought I'd ever go...as far as I could come.

When Korea came, I was one of the first to go. I flew south, south into that hellfire, it seemed south as far as a man could go, and then some.

At In Chon, we inched on into incredible cold and incredible fire-power. Once we were boxed in...trapped...I could show you on a map...in complete disarray, the unit, like a handful of islands tossed across the surface of the sea — cast from the same hand, you see, you could tell by the songs and uniforms, but one part split off from the other. Like islands.

A map, look here at this map of these islands; a map is like the words of a man — never quite what he really thinks but all you've got to go on.

I went on at In Chon with a great group of men at the beginning. Then, right there — as though someone had it charted from the start — right there at In Chon, the beginning ended. Beginning, during, and end of my war. End of the party, end of the last drunken song. As if I'd fought a war on a map and never quite seen what war really was.

I was hit nine times, upended, let me roll up this sleeve, look at the angle of the left leg between knee and ankle, upended in my beginning and sent flying over the mud, spraying blood like machine-gun fire, my body scattered over the battlefield like islands, the scars even now look to me like islands on the otherwise unbroken surface of a man who was pretty enough to appear on a poster all over America, and, I like to think, the world. Just so: my finger pointed at you. This finger of this right hand; I'm left-handed but what the hell. Uncle Sam Wants You.

That poster was a map for the destinies of many brave men. Many of them bought it when I was only...and so it goes.

And so I was hit nine, nine times—here, here, back here, and here, even in the nuts—no, no, I'm not going to show you. Obviously, I lived, I am alive before you in this hell-hole of the north, and not without gratitude. No, but it was a map of things to come.

Pain, drugs, nearness to death—it was a drunk, not a good one. Then waking, the world still looking as it looks when you look at it through something rolled up, like a map rolled up, and first hearing them say I'd never father children, and me just married, married in the war-joy, drunk on the shortness of time on a liberty just before I flew south over the Pacific and on in to In Chon.

I'd been gone only three weeks, a career marine to the bone, to the core, to the Corps, you might say, stopped dead (or near-dead), ended in my beginning. Stopped anyway nearly dead. Here I am before you, my memory no semblance really of reality, but a map of 53 years, but I appeared dead...to myself...and to others...who feared...I won't go into it, but still dream that I died, that I'm dead, that I'm dead and have been what should have been, now, a long time, that I died and all this, the north, had no beginning; it's not as vivid as it was, and it was so...damn this thing for which I have no word...so like edges ragged, sharp, defined, like pieces of grenade in a crater, blowing across expanse of dream, bits, almost of paper, parts of something like that poster, possibly a map, blowing across wastes of land and water...parts.

With time, concentration, and restricted vision, like looking at something through the hole of something like this map, rolled, a man can come to take—or mistake—a part for a whole.

Two years and more they filled half-killing me with tests and hospitals and x-ray maps of sore parts sewn back together before they discharged me, with honours, from the Corps, their saying I'd never father children flying across my consciousness like refrain from a song you wish you'd never heard, each word occurring sudden on the quiet surface of the mind's ear like an atoll on which you'd test a bomb.

And so, with dignity, with respect for the Corps, I appealed the discharge. And lost, and found out judge-advocates have their ways of sweeping aside fragments of the Corps said unable to father children. And the Corps found out I had my ways. I had a son (the little sonofabitch recently went federal evidence against some of the biggest dope money on the west coast...never mind that) and I appealed the discharge again...again I lost...reasons I won't go into.

My own father was on the Burma Road during the war. Not Korea. The one before. World War the second. On the Burma Road, the Lido Road, they called it, Army Airforce Engineers, he was a good man with maps, as engineers are. Had to explain to his brass his men yanking gold teeth from stiffs to buy oriental whores. Didn't drink. Didn't drink anymore than I do, except as he had to, you know, as I did, you know, with my men—he did, much the same, with his men.... They don't make men now as they did before, real men, men among men, you know what I mean: men who'll go balls-to-the-wall for what they believe. He'd never, my father, have the need to come or go north. Burma, they still called it Burma, like the shave-signs, they had it rough in Burma, took a lot of fire.

They sang the songs where they should have been sung. It was a good place to test who you were.

He was younger than some, but older than many more. For him, when he came home, the war of the world was ended forever. And it was so. The body of a world blown to hell was healed again, stitched up by peace... machine-gun-holes in the globe sewn over by sutures of word on pages of treaty.

I once went around with a woman, secretary, she could make a typewriter chatter like sten gun; after I married her, I never mentioned what her typing called to mind. She was the great find of my life, my wife was and always will be.

Well, I got rich, building contractor, once my drunk of soldiering ended. The son grew up and the wife wore down. Disease ended her, the son and I alone as never before.

No war, no wife, just money. After In Chon, like my father after Burma, I believed there couldn't be more war. My father had won. I was his son, I hadn't won my war exactly, but we had won, more or less, in Korea, Uncle Sam. Well, goddammit, I suppose, looking back, the line between winners and losers, by the time of Korea was getting blurry, I guess, but I was young and six-feet-four of hard-on to get to war. What son wouldn't want to say to his son: I won like my father before me.

And so, for me, as for my father, war was over forever and so I was wrong, as was he, wasn't reading the map right, and so on into the next war as far as deep and dirty as we could go: a war that stank so high that soldiers the age of my son, in rage, *fragged* their officers and come home or came north and bragged of it by way of re-aligning their compasses to their maps.

What goes around comes around and here we came boots-and-saddles, full-bore into the next stitch of war — like machine-gun-fire, the sound of the single shot lost in the sound of the rest, all the separate islands merging into a single expansive map of continuous war. Like sound from a rock and roll station: the end of one song overlapped by the beginning of the next.

And there were no songs. For Viet Nam. Plenty against but none for. Viet Nam. The big money made plenty of money selling the music of protest.

The son was a doper, not a soldier. To keep him alive and carrying the line, I sent him as far north as he could go.

So he came here and did whatever he did across borders for money — not for glory, not for flag, nor for beginning, nor for during, nor for ending anything begun by father and mother. He did what he found it necessary to do with little or no sense of before...as far as I know...there were no words, he didn't write...what I know I have only heard...from a source as reliable as this map, anyway...and this map has prevented my sinking this yacht in these waters.

Cornered, he copped out to the feds and sang his way free, so to speak, and they gave him cover and he lives wherever he lives under another name, one other than mine, the one you suppose that you know and don't and won't, but the one you call me by will serve as well as a map.

I don't know where he lives by another name. I could buy his whereabouts. He never wore a uniform. It wouldn't be the same.

The sameness of things got to me deep. I was rich and clean and a noteworthy citizen of what there was to be a citizen of and living no strategic terrain to be taken. Just a fucking map. Ever look closely at a map? Look at this edge, damn near as thin as the very air. Lift it up and look under. See? Nothing there.

The north, you know, is some like suicide; a man comes to it as a coward or a hero depending on what words are said by whom. And more: a going to north can be a going to war, just as necessary, as silly and phony and glorious — in the great drunken sense of that word: glorious.

I thought of suicide. All money, no pride, my wife dead, lots of women, all made of thin stuff, the son may as well have died. But I'm made of that yankee stuff that hates cowards who shoot themselves in hands and feet to buy their way out of the fire.

So I stayed in the bed I had made and continued building buildings I would have preferred to bomb and strafe instead.

It is said it takes an angry oyster to make a pearl. Shrapnel from the sea-battle invades the calm shell...you could map the shrapnel inside me still...they have on x-ray and cat-scan... man....Yes, an oyster there in his oyster bed just being one among others...man, there I was just one among others... until a single little grain of something...sand, they say, sand... suddenly makes what was comfort...intolerable; then...the animal...dies...or makes a pearl. Change your environment or change your life. Or both. Or kill one. I pity the sonsofbitches incapable of changing either, incapable of death or pearls.

And so, having thought of, then thought my way beyond the ending of my life...I suppose the bit of grit scouring around inside my shell that brought me out of hiding — I was disguised as a good citizen and it was an excellent disguise — the grit was pride, the almost perfect lack of it. It is maybe pride that makes us notice when we're nearly out of pride...or was in my case, having been, at least once, proud.

Inside, I knew there was something that longed for something: shells flying overhead, bits of bomb obliterating landscape, gunfire spurting the dirt around me, something, something...something more than being one more rich oyster in the oyster bed that whispers 'more...more...more' but never heard of the word 'enough'.

My young friend, I had had enough of more.

And so, since all maps end at one edge or another, I liquidated and went looking, age of fifty, good — maybe even great — citizen of half a century, took off looking for war...edgy as hell, but clearly at the end of a map...took off.

Not north. Not then. But now...after three years...of war.

And chance had me in its sights...or had me mapped all along, depending how you look at it. Most don't look at all...ever...I did...and found my way, by chance, in my kid...not exactly; that is, it was nothing he said...more of what he did, or was doing, gave me an idea (same idea, different scale), his small-time dope commerce across the border to survive without working, unlike his old man, without becoming a clam, an oyster in the oyster bed. He doesn't know my whereabouts any more than I know his...any more than you can see North Island from Moresby...except on this map, these shapes...the kid is just a shape I remember.

Terrible drain...cocaine...booze, the whole drug thing. A man is different from lower animals in that he has to get high...different from those gulls there, different from that rock full of sea-lions we spooked yesterday...high, no way to deny that...but it's no high if you don't have your senses intact... can't be high and drunk at the same time, no high when you're full of booze or cocaine.

And I don't buy the hippie crap about natural high, not exactly...the love-beaded bastards in their uniforms are as bad as the goddamn F.B.I. in their J. Edgar Hoover blue suits. You got to get high on something...like a war, yeah, a war... something that takes all your consciousness and translates it into something you can see: hunk of sculpture...a skyscraper, maybe...a castle that has stood for a thousand years, wiped out in an instant by a bomb...direct hit...it's all the same: action, result, something you can see, result by whatever name. War is no tragedy. We've been putting up cities and knocking them down forever. Bombing is an action. Rebuilding is an action. It keeps the dying animal called man living.

What else has a man to do with his time while he dies...other than go play in the death and try to keep from being killed while he plays?

A long, green laze low over the windless, blue pools of days. All the pater-noster ponds downpour toward the silt-fans of an imperious delta.

The red whales are not on fire. Sunset. Or a coloured filter between the light and the world.

Moon-fangled dolphins crescent toward the centre of the sea where light is still a black vacuole.

The ones going as far north as they can go, some pursued, some in pursuit, will pay little attention.

The north waits to burn and they will poke the small lanterns of their two certainties into the moving corners of the northern dark.

But the days littered with black minutes have begun. The skull is an interruption of breeze. Behind the eyes, ashes sift into soft dunes.

Blood the hound-figured holocaust.

The trees of the heavens and the trees of corporeity burn inequally.

The trees of hell: nonflammable.

Satiety is a small unchartered isle in the orange, open ocean of the hunger.

My time is of the old trees: dangerous, unstable, combusts quickly. Near others.

Any scientist will tell you things burn best in the mist.

The fish which light the sea at night are not mere phosphor turning, and the water is not boiling when the stream-green goes red with fins and flames.

Call it oxidation, disarm it, call it rot, then explain slowly, clearly, and decisively to yourself that this is the organic, the cycle, perfection.

And the oily ashes of the fish will save you.

A large fire at the centre.

Weak fires around the circumference where darkness ends and skin begins.

From here where the scorpion self-strikes, to log to log, following the air, things burn on in toward the hotter hub, toward the place where, possibly, light begins. And lives.

But the centre is too everywhere and too, too however.

There are at least two choices: to peer into or pass through the mirror of ashes.

The embering logs of the vanished give the disfigured slopes of what is to come.

There might have been walls, at least, and a roof between us and the rain. Nothing came to hand but the burning.

No name for what passed here.

We left only frames of windows and doors too open upon the precincts where how to forget grew. Where the stunted saplings of perhaps later are beginning to appear.

We turn, with the last droplets of fuel away and away to might have been possible. Otherwise.

I burned up my space in a beach fire which warmed no one.

At the *marge* of the dark / light, there was no voice drunkenly singing.

Once I mistook the clench of flames for something other: a distant harmonica, perhaps white foam on a black rock burning dry.

The fear of being misunderstood: it burns well.

The fear of being understood burns better.

There are ten billion burning cells on each side of the burning brain, each cell with as many as ten thousand burning endings.

For the fear of being ignored, I can neither ignite nor extinguish.

A day is a high pile of breaker-beaten wood—dry, waiting for high hazard...or lightning.

Sleep until it's alright.

The idea, for no reason, begins to burn. Sleep or flame inhales all the pilings of all possible wharves.

One awakens from one dream into another like ascending a burning building storey by storey.

The four corners of sleep heat and curl until the daylight drops and the smoke goes the colours of darkness.

All the cargo craft will come aground or anchor out too far until the flames strangle, only the orange edges remain, and the squeak of substance giving.

In a city of masts and fumes, I observe a man ablaze in a crowd whose edges I cannot see.

Those near him catch fire, head first, bend, twist, blacken —then go out.

Inside the river, rocks roll over and disclose their dark, wet unders.

Beneath them, everything dies of travel and light.

Look up. Check the geese. Go the other way.

In a fury of ink and chilly colour change, the small octopus
jetted into me.

Then grew.

What it fed upon, I never knew until far too late.

It takes me to wait beneath rocks in low-tide pools between
the go and go of world.

When the darkness appears just a little darker than it should, go
liquid, it is only the whale rising.

The biggest beast is not unexpected; the instant of arrival is
surprising.

Go liquid.

Get darker than the dark.

When, unexpectedly, the largest darkness is rising darker
than all darkness should, the ice floe is breaking up instead of
merely melting.

Swallow the water.

The whale is smaller than water.

Swallow.

And so it is the case of the cameraman and the avalanche.

The perfect mutual understanding.

The white mountain will fall as he films it and kill him.

To the last he will continue filming.

Beneath oil, slash, tailing piles, and bones of caribou, we buried the north together. Only a little bewildered cold remains to ghost the grave-side.

When N falls from the compass-face, all other directions merge.

୬

Learn your own water. A lake or a river. One water is enough. You can have a bay, a cove is better.

No man can handle a sea.

୬

Never learn to swim. It only prolongs the drowning.

୬

They unlocked your middle beneath the artificial light. Opened your darkness. Thereafter, you carried that light everywhere, the ghostly glow moving over ghostly snow.

The drugs which supplanted your blood against the harbour dolphin pain did not deaden the animal. Simply your gigantic body, hallucinated to a neutral corner of the convalescent room, continued to surge against the storm-surf of sickness.

୬

The interstices between laughter are filled with madness
merely: ignition, moving away from the plane of solid earth,
velocity rising, stage after stage, jettison, parts falling back into
the black, damaged sky.

    Space shuts about you like an envelope about a letter in
which it has all been said.

It is a wrong day for the fish. Ignore the sun. Do not reach
for the boat on the truck-top rack. It will be a long time before
they find the black-fly-coated deadshape lying among waves of
the marsh-grass.

The white-spider aurora stood over us that first night you
gave us the hobo canon as tramp-philosopher-king, and fish
fried hobo-wise in the open, and tea from a pitch-blackened
gallon can.

Own nothing.

When I touch selected surfaces: carved soapstone, certain places of uncertain women, dark argillite curve, the grip of a tool by flesh worn smooth: my fingertips do what my eyes do when they stare.

I am speaking to you with my death between us. Fabric of it resembles neither Nile Valley gauze nor the sacred confessional screen.

Mind and apparency have carried me through this narrows of endless ends of time.

Words are always behind instead of before me because of time's bungled quality. When last was I a single word travelling among others. That was my desire: one molecule of something more general, more in the manner of a long, moody current, more like a tide of blue cobra hooding a shore. Not, certainly not, instead: correspondence between one pebble and more than one wind.

Any death is a death if blood and brain agree to say so.

I am speaking to me through cellophane. I come towing a message for secrets forever sealed.

A death knows of time only rumour. Each must instruct his death in protocol, each in his manner, in order to assist not-death in its efforts to be. Each elucidation: the length of a life, precisely.

For the moment, I believe this, as I have almost believed almost all my lies at one telling or another.

A few I have believed more than once.

Some, only partly. And not often.

When death succeeds life as monarch of superstitions, one must back-stalk all the truths he has talked and, one by one, unbelieve them.

To summon nothing, eliminate something. That *certain something* will become certain nothing in or outside time.

The shrinking tree of the spine passes from vertical to bow beneath the weight of wind. Heavy moss chandeliers darken the white yardarms of bone.

Carefully I lift one corner of the sea to spy the mongrel asleep beneath. Unlike me, the animal is not sleeping beyond the death of his essential dog.

Attempt to invent a whole from this part of light travelling across the insensate sea-skin of art.

I am speaking to you from here behind.

From here: right here: between these lines.

From here where voice forges in the foundry of absence.

Before me. Incising all the new water. My old wake.

ع‌‌ے

Elk rising like land-whales on the surface of the willow and
salal sea.

ع‌‌ے

The silence mouths a far-off splash across north island darkness
which segues to darkness of a Carolina swamp quarter of a
century ago, different moss draped from different trees, same
splash.

ع‌‌ے

Silt-clouds in the current: there is yet someone upstream.

ع‌‌ے

Dream of zebras. Grove of zebras growing across a wide plain.
Long, gloomy hesitations between animals.

ع‌‌ے

At the sting of the barb, I roll on the surface. Join face of water
to face of air. But light tackle holds and the dream-murder
holds.

ع‌‌ے

Someone hunkers over a fire blowing the coals of all that
has burned.

ع‌‌ے

The sound of water comes for me, but I promise me the fish haven't yet entered the upstream of my breath.

૨ફ

I strip in and cast out the suddenly awkward line like one struggling to remember the last of a long dream.

૨ફ

She explodes awake as if consciousness were a thing to take by violence and surprise.

૨ફ

Death is more sudden where high wind sharpens the blades of shallow water.

૨ફ

The blunted stumps of these driftlogs contain all weather.

૨ફ

This deadly disjunct. Between what little I describe and what all I have seen.

૨ફ

What lives in time only. The opposite of glaciers bellowing across the dark.

૨ફ

The times of terror without cause are with me always. Sleepwalking. Or waiting at the next fork in the shadow of a fern. Possibly lower: within the gills of a mushroom which is nourishing. Or deadly. Depending.

ॐ

The transparent life is not always invisible among other lives.

ॐ

In the summer place of north, sheets cover the furniture. Strata of dust cover the sheets.

ॐ

My question is a lone horseman patroling a horizon of voices.

ॐ

This is a sad sandwich, in bed here, we three: you and I and my mind.

ॐ

Lichen of the vegetable mask wears through to the granite of our impassable pasts.

ॐ

The bridges we build between word and thing have always been collapsing. Therein lies the hope.

Hope is a blind, white fish deep in an Ozark cave.

Fog like a leg gone to sleep.

North is a journey to the centre of the onion.

In the mind-light of braiding river time, I was a minor incident between no longer and not yet.

Follow this way through the dark curtain of rain. It will take you to his cabin. It is the only one there, you can't miss it, there on the edge where yes and no contiguate. There may or may not be a light on. If not, think in tungsten: the filament burnt far too soon for the price, but the vacuum still perfectly performing. Inside it is dry. Stay the night or part of it. The roof sags with weight of moss and wet. The structure is not as old as it looks. Here, weather accounts for virtually everything.

Here, beyond the small sand mountain at the edge of the reserve, time tilts diagonal. Ordinary turns unusual. Certainty comes over me that this windy light is nowhere but here...and like...nothing...other than whatever it appears...to me... right now...right here. As if from somewhere above, excarnate, I see me seated on the third silvered step before the carver's home watching consciousness embody as breeze in the dune-grass flow.

That dried black crap hanging up there above the stove? Seaweed. Indian food. Make you fart like an old dog. It's good for you. You white guys don't fart enough. There's an old saying up here: Never follow a Haida into a pub toilet in seaweed season.

*Mind this: stick to the driftwood when you screw around up
near the spit, eh? Stay off the beach and out of those marsh
meadows where they graze. They can't handle the footing on
the driftwood; that rubbish will save your skin. The farmers
brought them. Then went tits up and left everything. Turned
them loose to survive if they could. That herd of wild cattle has
been growing since turn of the century. More than one dummy
has bought it who mistook them for tame.* Smoking, safe here
atop the sea's graveyard for logs and trees, it comes to me what
occurs when a life domesticized first faces what seems
simultaneously like itself and strange. Smoke rises as the mist
descends. I'm searching both sides of the interior drift: for
anything which, in any case whatsoever, might revert. To
anything. At all.

With his back to the lakeface going zebra with evening westerly
and dark, he flattens his hands before him against the
window-pane of heat:

*They was no anglo and frog Canadian bullshit among us
tramps. Tramp is no bum. They was no work. More bums
today than they was back then. This big nort' used to be good
for not much more than campsite for hobos like me—place to git
healty, live on fish, mingle a little wit the trees, get your mind
off the Depression, and hunker like this by a fire like this, by the
hole a good fire poke in the night. A lot of good nights like
this... tell... stories. Ashes from all them fires blown away
now into that silence where everything before right now
blows... east, maybe... heh, heh, haw, Christ.... This is no
camp compared to them camps. People like you camp for
novelty, not to keep alive, keep warm, keep dry. Camp, for
you, is like a wharf: not your life: just... eh... attached to it.
Me, it's the other way around.*

If the weather get owly enough, you'll go find a motel.
Wasn't no motels then.
   Not much place to be alone now.
   Depression free a man forever or scare him into a citizen.
   Hope I croak before I ain't no more no hobo.

It's an old picture, be careful, no, go ahead, count 'em,
twenty-seven men standing on that stump. Not many of those
left now. Trees like that. Loggers like that. Only a few of us
know where they are, the trees. Never worry about the big
weeds on the claim, but stay away from the pole show. The
little ones, they look harmless, undercut and drop 'em with a
few revs of the saw. But they walk on you, barber-chair on you,
they come down quick: the whole tree, drive you into the mud
like a nail. Rotten stuff from up top of the big spruce and cedar
comes down slow and noisy. You got time to look up and
shag ass.
   In the toothpicks, you're under before you hear your breath
go out.

Inside me at the shore of the frozen lake they are still talking.
   We shouted, shouted, waved our dim lanterns over the snow.
I feel him riding through the darkness over the ice.
   They say the centre is a deep unfreezing maw. Beneath the
horse the ice mumbles and moans.
   The hag scratches and suspects. Through her vague snow of
remembered disappointments, she curses him laughing in a
warm room up the shore.

Won't he go round, the boy began. Eyes like frozen lakes with dark centres stopped him short.

This is one of many, many villages snowed apart around a frozen lake.

In the spring, gone are ice, ice village, eye-like frozen lake. And ice riders riding over the ice through the dark.

It is winter, I listen into the wind for hooves, for a splash, for a shout.

I dream of Roethke reportedly: of driving a long writing out a narrowing tentacle over the hard sand, pea-gravel, then dune-powder toward the spit's end between two deadly waters, until the breakers booze against both sides, plant-life behind me, high wind always, sea-otter, seal, sea-lion, be with me, but a few feet away, be my left and right, bobbing between my opposing streams, as I go gorgeous to surface blasting rainbow over the margin in the motions of your dolphin and my whale.

In the thrashed and half-buried crabtraps of the inside coves, visible at low and minus, the bait is gone. But not the evidence. Nor the whale. Remaining are the hard, empty skins of life that entered the easy labyrinth here, but could not exit, nor exist.

Behind me ceased the tree-line. There was thunder. Here at land's vanish, I only see instead of remember. Along the way, bodies of log thrown high and askew, the good surface gave way, pea-gravel and powder-sand swallowed all my axles. I only remember instead of see.

On whose coasts lie my lost oaken hatch-covers? Whose swilling bilges spat these filthy blots upon my dream and pristine beaches? Wind and moon collude.

I am, I might have been, I was: amber agate sprung from bubbles of sea-floor basalt, twitched free by nerves of tide, then polished to idiot glitter by machine.

Wild cattle of the muskeg pursue me high onto my driftwood. Every year, stronger, swifter, they grow. Nimbleness and speed fall away from me like faces of sand bluff under the rain.

Now and then a black bull, ancient, dead upon the dead trees, neck broken, bloated, eyes consigned to eagles and to tides. And now and then the bust of a black-tail buck, above on the sea-cliff, a too-clear silhouette against the falling fog.

Naw, if anyone saw, no one would admit to it... Right over there... You can over and see the stumps for yourself... Smack in the middle of the Second War, The Japs sneaked in past Masset at night, Then steamed right down Masset Inlet here, pretty as you please.

They cut a boat-load of airplane spruce... Best in the world up here... Then they F.O.'ed home to Tokyo to make zeros... They say once... but you know they did it plenty of times... Nobody heard anything about it until quite a while after the war.

Whispers live still between the logs which shape the vacancies of this unremembered shelter.

As rot returns this all to wilderness, the voices of rain become less legible.

A thought like a small rodent spirits through a fault of dim memory and goes to repose in the shadow of a sardine-can ashtray in one corner.

The room remembered much until its spine overhead gave in against the wind that batters down a will.

Sea otter carry the uncertain remainder of the species within. Their days rise and die like minus tides beneath moonfire. Before the forces of greed and water, they change. Like sea-jungle. Like the underwater streaming of fur.

I am weather; where I go, sunlight is always subsiding. Skin resists for a while; then the rain falls inside me. When the sun again comes, water goes up, goes away. Not greener for the cycle, I stay.

Gentian light domes the opaline inlet. Each instant: a diatom of difference. And the eyes of the word never quite enough exact to fix the change.

This vista, too, I shall complicate.

Beyond word memory, before the profligate fish runs which cloud the clear currents of survival with leisure, earlier than the art of ovoid and canoe-form, than cedar seacraft and the widening Haida eye, we trouble the chill sand, hungry continuously, fearing presence and absence of forest, fearing all secrets and all knowledge of the sea.

A day is what this amounts to. As cold amounts to cold. Cold comes in shapes of drift and stone and attaches to places of skin, imperfectly numb.

This line of beach was drawn by no draftsman, flow as it does like the hem of something rain-green, dropped by something in escape from form.

We don't discuss this. Nor any other matter. Where we are belongs only incidentally to the round or the flat or the neither.

Thirty thousand years hence, some will insist our because was a hole, a flaw in an age of ice. Some will call them liars.

Nothing will remember us but our middens. Basalt cores. The stone blades we chipped from them to part shell from shell.

We fear, therefore we worship. Or might worship, were there time.

Whether language, whether law, whether tradition, whether art, even minimal: no legacy.

Instead of the embarrassing load of history, we have, inedible as it is, our circuminsular mobility.

Their onus will be to invent us from these spalls of rock thirty thousand years after. There will be time then for idleness, art, nonchalant destruction.

Starvation can settle all art and war.

Flakes of clam and mussel shell will talk. Not clearly. They prefigure tailing piles and birdless slash.

Volcanic blades from volcanic cores, we leave these and nothing more to speak for us. A brittle tool between thumb and first finger, daylong worrying the thing between shells, working to yawn something self-buried and self-closed. A starving mind wedges between two lines and pries.

When the well-fed ones arrive to replace us, no resistance. There has been neither time nor occasion to prepare an etiquette of war.

Possibly a tribe without destination is prideless. Possibly without even a word for pride. Possibly we leave the births, the deaths and the other occasions to remember behind among their moist and empty shells. Possibly bad and good have not yet crossed the water to us. Possibly they would never solve the distance between feeding and not feeding.

Where pride, guilt. Where guilt, rage for history. As bivalves comprehend guilt, thus do we.

Yesterday smells, in a general way, exactly of today.

Thought cannot exceed the hours of light and a few fire-eyed suspicions of the dark.

Thirty thousand years from this, their present too cluttered with future to inhabit, some will turn imagination toward one of our days.

Far from the hinge of survival, they will think of nothing more useful to do with whole lives, much less days.

Dream us merely a moving then, a moving among the weave of winds, close to ice constantly, naked or nearly naked, herded by whims of light, the same food going wary and elusive, place to place, copulation when there's energy for recreation, the trudge again afterwards, frequently a wasted birth, death commonplace, weather permitting and never permitting... unused time to rest the mind against an exposed boulder at low tide.

The situation is far too spare for an eye to stop and prefer one stone from among all visible stones.

No messenger has arrived to explain we won't be here still gouging the sand for clams, come thirty thousand years.

That quiet little kid a while ago? My nephew. You watch what he did when he came in the door? Always does it. Scares hell out of me. When my dad was alive, he used to come in the door and, without saying anything to anybody, go to my work table over there and examine my stuff in argillite. Wouldn't even say hello until he looked at every piece. The little kid, step for step, does exactly the same thing. He wasn't yet alive when my father died. I'm not really religious; probably I'm less superstitious than those guys at the stock market. My dad is dead. And yet....Like my dad, there's something about the way he eyes an argillite blank. Deeper than the surface of the clay...as if there's something in there to talk to.

*The damn logging outfits don't now what they're doing and
they won't listen. . .just like the damn anthropologists who
know everything before they come to tell indians what an indian
is; we sit around making up bullshit lies to answer their damn
fool questions. The loggers won't listen when you warn them.
For example: everybody knows that each of the islands is
fastened to the bottom of the ocean by the roots of one giant
spruce; six, maybe seven hundred years old. You fall one of
them anchor trees and the island will drift off anywhere. If the
Japs found out, they'd come tow this island to Tokyo. You got
any idea how tough it is to navigate an island this size? No
matter how hard you argue, damn anthropologists convince
themselves that totem poles tell stories and that somewhere
there's a Haida hiding who has the key to Haida secrets. Christ,
the damn things are ornamental. Heraldry. Like a coat-of-arms,
except that it grows with each potlatch. The chief acquires
more names and more totems. The more property he gives
away, the greater his status. Christ, the whole bloody society is
based on sex, food, property, pride, greed, warfare and
slavery—just like yours.*

A metabolism gone as still as stone, seemingly not breathing,
silent heart ringing anvil blows through tiny bones: this fawn
sequestered here in shallow grass, the doe seeing from
somewhere I do not see as the fingers of my right hand escape
contact with judgement and make contact with the russet fur of
a life only just begun.

As the hand returns to me, thought flashes that the doe will
never return.

The transparent skin of my scent — odourless to me —
subtracts this animal from both origin and future.

In the course of almost forty years' passage from one precinct
of desert to another, where else has the stink of my finger-prints
made septic the unspoiled?

I, who accept that beauty is nothing if not untouchable.

I, whose touch, nevertheless, has browned the petals of many
gardenias.

This rising river of answers because I have no Haida questions.

From buried adzes, from a broken yew bow, from strata of
shell, they set forth to resuscitate the past ... or join
it ... exactly as it never was, exactly as it never would have
been.

Something not yet reported lost is dying with difficulty.
Starving.

Hoar-frost whiskers the weather-silvered planking of the
wharf. The wharf begins to trouble me, hinged as it is to the
edge of the end of land, centipede feet poised on the surface of
water, a thing incomplete in wait for the return of something
incomplete.

Consciousness nervously blows the pages of memory: The
Wanderer...*læna*...lone with o rich and long-drawn-
out...*læna*....
The urge to speak of this to someone.
If there was ever anyone, he is missing. And hungry.
At the end of the wharf, even more unease: the aspect of my
footprints, dark in light frost, both following, both leading one
another in one direction only.

I was a man who trespassed this land when a mirage of
unknown still dwelt in the small of his hand.

One could come, here, to a death of wrath.
To wrath seeping out an uncaulked aperture and all bilge
vacuums broken.
The calendar goes end-up and subsides.
No ship on any horizon.
The moongoggled surface of the locofoco sea.

This carving was one of numberless lights in the blood.
The work complies with vision only as body complies
with soul.
Body: the sad sack of skin stuffed with death and
carnival prizes.

The icecap of knowing somewhat remits.

Dawn features of isle topography like dice cast over the green crap-table surface of the sea by an idle deity.

If not islands, then my register of islands.

On this imperfect skeleton, cure a skin of a few even less perfect lines.

Shipwreck of one of the huge ideas upon an impassable but irresistable reef of language.

Rainbows of fish take up residence and thrive in the derelict hull.

In time, any massive failure can ease under the surface of memory, the glare light of guilt scarring the dark all the way down.

The difference between new and used is useless inside the sea.

Once, the new hulk was an astounding strangeness sinking through the bottomless familiar.

The droplet trapped in the spider skein rocks in thin breeze like a bell which, with every knell, loses presence in the tactile photograph.

Come, Evening: bronze light at the westmost coast of all there is to know.

Light gears down.

The photographer seen between filaments of spider-goods bursts into a frenzy of wrong lenses—without sense that there are focal lengths of fate no lens will accommodate.

Among these silks of shadow, the hands, my hands of water, cannot hold fast any longer.

Capacity to dream an absolute shape of island without means to awaken within it.

Infrequently, rage for an open place, for the camouflage of visibility.

Gearing of my insular season engages teeth of the pinion. Sap is stirring in the deadliest trees.

To escape the island sickness, travel to the horizon, turn left.

Melting light.

A tawn floating toward the ridge-top, very long shot,
*Woman, nobody shoots off-hand at three bloody hundred
yards. Not even a man*, cross-hairs seem to twitch within their
circle of collapsing evening.

*Settle down and listen: this is about eating.... Killing is the
eldest (and probably most constant) human skill.... You put
out that old buck's lights, Lady, you offed him and he never
knew a thing. If you kill, kill with style as you did just now.*

*The lousy part of hunting is that the shooter can somewhat
initiate but never fully be the time-free beauty of the kill.*

The sudden, umbral bloom of sound widens away in a
bird-flight of echo.

The strata of silence will recover.

Changed.

Agate from pores of a basalt seafloor fall to the beach over the
shoulder of a shovelling tide.

When the day tilts westward, just after a fine rain, after
tongues of the Hecate dragon have wearied of flicking the coast
with froth and flotsam, at a precise slant of sunbreak—an
octopus motionless and scarcely changing colour in its
boulder-pool—, then: sight pans to the lacework of crystalline
lights strewn across the water-tattooed sand.

Unlinked from mind, the hand begins collecting. Objects
heavy and unaesthetic as random can make them. Useless and
beautiful, merely, when wet.

Vertical wind, horizontal rain, the affair of warm Japanese
current with the air of Alaskan ice.
Here the atmospheric face of a continent is shaped.
Configurations of cloud change from thought to thunder.
At the centre, space more slowly swirls inside outer time.
Senses archive what the will will not.
Plethora and high summer chill.

The high-rigger tops a home-tree.
Then falls with the crown of this plant with which six
centuries have not dared meddle.
On his way down, he finds, for the first time, he can plot
with absolute accuracy the progress of each travelling part
of his body.

Caution near the ones like winter eagles who pause atop only
the most high places and glare through the dustless distances.

Stonestroke.

Finally, cutting has whittled to a reason: simply to fondle this love for sharpening.

I glance up through the labour's glow—heavens bloody as the business down below. Across the battlefields of logging-slash: only cedar snags. So many, too many, deathtimes still standing.

With each ingenius stroke of steel on stone, ascending toward Hell's grace.

The stain of borrowed time does not wash nor wear free from the fragile fabric of the underbrain.

Sometimes, one dreams, it charms against the sickness of not living.

This dream of a captive will letting go: an old and huge sailing craft, loosed from mooring, stiffly shouldering the rollers, under full sail, in full blundering lurch toward open sea.

Then: a lone spinnaker bloom which flaws the otherwise perfect curve of horizon.

Lost is another word for ordinary in ordinary insular speech. Islands within the islands will never be mapped. Notion of proportion is small salvation when lost in the head-high salal. While the continuous coast erases and rewrites itself, remember: any river is a system which subdivides not-river into all not-river outside the river and all the rest of the non-river which is inside the river itself. System explains no other system. Never is a river more than river. Lost is yet another system which declines to self-explain.

More than geography removed: of her, I remember only eye-light. The inerrant dim of an execution chamber. And, like white land birds blooming from an open hamper, will, releasing and releasing. I arrive at the stations of the hours as usual with too much baggage. And immensely over prepared.

Easy, the thought gone dancing to celebrate, the thought gone dancing only to dance, that thought turned dimly, dimly more drunken, a thought entering the wide night for just a little unsmoked air, fresher, very much fresher now, strolling more and more steadily down the frost-whiskered wharf, constellations in this bush place inhaling the eyes, the good sound of solo footsteps on heavy wood ringing out to break against the banks of water-noise to either side. Then the better drunkeness in the best dark at the wharf's end where the sea is seen only by ear, then the phosphor imp, the urge to dive and swim to shore, reappear a quenched clown at the music... *can't be even a hundred yards between the end of the road and the end of the wharf there. Less from the beach to the end of the wharf depending on your tide. You got maybe twenty seconds this time of year. No one's made it back to beach that anyone remembers. Happens all the goddam time.*

Gauze sky of a maker contemplates its fake in the one-way mirror of sea.

There comes to me nothing to say on behalf of space squandered in search for a primal wilderness.

Fingerprints now cover everything dreamworthy and soon the whole of the galaxy will be second-hand.

These subdued fields cleared by others, I till them always with the thinning hope I'll one day awaken and find them grown up around me—for the first time wild.

I've come here to salvage, to terrorize a consciousness, sunken, hugely encrusted in urban coma.

I surround it with peaceless water, then whisper: *You cannot swim, don't even dream of it. Summon the last of your small cunning. Become invisible. Become island unnoticed among islands. Think east to the far edge of survival. Think west to a lout defacing blank leisure with form.*

A peregrine drops from indigo eternity toward a small animal fleeing in every direction—never before thus bone-frightened, never before thus expansively alive.

For him, parts of island remain tidily *as though* until he breaks parts of his body against them.

Until he breaks his mind against them, the absences exist and exist.

Tlell:

Light goes irresolute and slow, when it shows, and time concealed deep in the light.

In commerce, immense significance is a laminate of details which, considered singly, seem trivial.

They are.

Great whales acquire their stupendous lives inhaling plankton whose tiny lives seem negligible in their invisibility.

They are.

Night set. Remembrance of the future in wrath: this chisel is chief among tools of every significant liar. Light pumices all surfaces at the high slack tide of sight. That the spangled fish are in to spawn is never altogether definite. The nets remain, in any case, at ready. What has finally been abandoned becomes an antique photograph, its worth never expressed in a speech of quality, but in one of oblique history. Surface floats fire the nervous murk with phorphorous in an easy crescent of tireless waiting. Deeper sparks along the line signal it is all very nearly over.

To this the spooked hope has come: the spell of glacial refugium: a single spit of thought untouched by the last and everlasting cape of ice.

On the evidence of flora nonexistent elsewhere on the skin of the orb. Mushrooms, especially, their changes in the short north summer dark.

On the evidence of certain greens of uncertain moss.
On the evidence of swamp in flames of fern almost
impossible to cross.
On the evidence of desire for beyond what hangs from the
cedar as certainty.
Transit. Sick. Inglorious.
Noli me tangere. Just in case.
Remain far back. Try to go away.

Inscribed in pause: fume and wisp of word float through one
another with none the wiser.

Almost love of a kind for the animals and trees warily enters
my hands.
And feeling, definite feeling, for trumpeting, behemoth
machines dreamt and driven by old children.
For those who stand tall and speak loudly for geese or for the
teeth of gears: nothing in me stirs.

Never again call me painter. I am without imagination.
Incapable of invention. I only trace. That much, surely, even
you can see. I commit to canvas only what is revealed to me.

I was numerous figures of time at the flumes.

I watched the portions hiss from height to stream until watched and watcher fused and appeared one thing.

In recall, trees arise again over war-killed slopes of thought to supervise gravity bearing me, part after part, mostly water, back down to water, compounding with all other flux of *lux*: the grand translation of the works into the mother tongue of endlessly abiding sea.

I am learning slowly to prefer there were never trees, no hand, no tool to hew them down, never water, never dangerous ways down inscribed by rampaging gravity.

I focus on the cool, smooth flumes: the light upon their lines which bear nothing between nowhere and nowhere.

What I need is what I have but no longer see.

Satana, the cryogene, so easily outstares time at the beatless heart of Hell.

The doors of gods are closed tight tonight.

Trestles of law, beneath their weight of revision, collapse.

Like those of mortal order, the doors of gods are, tonight, tightly closed.

From the time I entered north, I have been a magnet for bears. I extract them from even the smallest wilderness.

It is as though they know I have killed their kind and would kill my own with small encouragement.

As if to compare two destructive forces, they dare almost anything — except passage between my obsession and its custodian.

The golden goose-horn of eternity.

Pilgrim, make your peace with Time or seize scrotum and honk the heavens deafeningly.

I have availed myself of heat, of light, near the blaze of your big burning.

Gratefully.

But when your awaited sinking comes, as your unusual vessel detaches from its wharf of unbroken floating,

As you extinguish, as you go down light by light, I intend to be a long, long darkness away.

Here at the frontier, it turns suddenly the wrong weather for those who fear darkness most during the day.

Indeed there is a personal god up there. And nosey.

A god of love triangulates on hate for love of useless symmetry.

Only poets, the sonofabitch hates, more than it hates poetry.

Interregnum between the twin lanterns of dusk and dark.

Between what it has come to and what it might have been.
How long is the dark, Dad?
Sleep as fast as you can.

Mind well-balanced on one leg: old heron, an older swamp, both dozing.

At some point, all tropes turn and vanish. Somewhere. The words, quite simply, must stop.

Somewhere.

Toward pure purpose:

To pound this icy stake of shape through the brass heartworks of snicking time.

Newcomer, take note of this: here the drunken eagle flies with impunity.

Who banishes himself to north necessarily leaves behind all state occasions of the mind.

Memory, the unerring golden retriever, incurable of toothing
the quarry beyond, almost, identity.

A cage of white mainland birds, long captive, unexpectedly
freed. Will, thus, releases will. Releases. A will letting go.
Will releasing.

These words against the darkness from which these words
are carved.

These silences against the black fire inside which all silence
forges.

So gracefully silent eternity shrills silence at the tiny,
temporal thrash.

The situation of fishing explains me: my high-seas trawlers, the big draggers, ravaging my seafloors; my seine-boats with their transparent nets of consciousness, ceaselessly sifting aqueous space; fewer and fewer the gillnetters now; and so with the solo trollers, their gear suggestive of seabirds drying their wings.

This persists: one man clinging to a cliff-face over the water, spear drawn. Waiting. Forever, if necessary.

Gale winter raindark and only this wharf not listing.

Someplace in the distance, the very distance is listening.

The telephone man: Instead of routineing toward Juskatla and the radio repair shack, the truck insists north toward Masset, but slows and pulls in at the road to the abandoned farm because of a particular strong and naked deciduous tree towering there in memory. As he climbs out, undresses, and folds each article neatly on the seat, he looks across the slope of the lumpy meadow: 'I wonder why no one uses this as site to shoot clay pigeons.' Stark naked, he pulls on his boots again, clamps on climbing spurs, removes a length of rope with a knot at one end whose configuration calls to mind a venerable tradition. Expertly, as if it were communications wire, he coils then slips the circle over his right shoulder. The exact branch is high enough, substantial, he is certain, as he ascends the early morning.

Almost mint, I entered my interior rainscape. I left it a junk place for huge things no longer used. There has never been another way. And there won't.

I was up foreward. She was in the galley fixing the grub. The campstove flared. I could see fire through the windshield of the troller and hurried back. When I put it out with the extinguisher, I looked around to say something. She was gone. Must have lit out for the aft of the boat and run overboard. Eight-knot current there in the channel. Too damn cold. Up here no one learns how to swim. We can't marry within the band. Had to go Alaska to find her.

A hamper of white mainland birds suddenly freed: Will releases, releases. The will releasing.

She spent the time of her life insular, deliberating what might be worthy of her time.

Because north is nearest nothing, again and again I come back, searching. This is the country where souls, more and more foreign to one another, dwell in uneasy exile.

The glare sea of excess truth now surrounds my used residue of mystery: it has closed it to all other unknowns and continues closing. By the instant, my inside island is less. I am the next ice age advancing.

I am dead when my senses close the shutters. There have been entirely too many lives.

It is said it was a death-drive
Extincted us—
All prodded, stupid, bewildered,
Gregarious into the sea. Also said:
Haida hunters shot the remaining two.
Some say we were
The only mammal native here,
Whatever native comes to mean.
    Now gone
And everywhere
As only things long gone can do.
We await your arrival
At a place you once dreamt up in fright.
    Yours truly,
The Dawson Caribou.

I am
Where lost things go
Until they are
And never
Found.

ACKNOWLEDGEMENTS

Poetry (Chicago), *Tamarack*, *New Orleans Review*, *Open Places*, *Poetry Canada Review*, *Prism International*, *Northward Journal*, *The Lunatic Review*, *Greenfield Review*, *West Coast Review*, *Event*, *Poetry Australia*, *Interstate*, *Vancouver Literary News*.

Part of this manuscript won 'runner-up' in the CBC Literary Competition and was broadcast on 'Anthology' and 'The Hornby Collection.'

Spiral of Mirrors
Hunt in an Unmapped Interior
Canticle for Electronic Music
Man in the Glass Octopus
The Great Bear Lake Meditations
Parallax
Contemporary Poetry of British Columbia (editor)
*Volvox: Poetry From The Unofficial Languages of Canada
   in English Translation* (editor)
Night Freight
Nothing Speaks for the Blue Moraines
Quarks: Three Plays
Breath of the Snow Leopard
The Qualicum Physics
Esox Nobilior Non Esox Lucius
Fazes in Elsewhen
Fugue Brancusi
Various Northerly Meditations

RECENT TITLES IN THE PENUMBRA PRESS POETRY SERIES

ANN FOX CHANDONNET *Auras Tendrils (Poems of the North)*
    ISBN 0 920806 45 7

DEBORAH GODIN *Stranded in Terra*
    ISBN 0 920806 53 8

MARY WEYMARK GOSS *In Hiding*
    ISBN 0 920806 54 6

NEILE GRAHAM *Seven Robins*
    ISBN 0 920806 55 4

M.T. KELLY *Country You Can't Walk In and Other Poems*
    ISBN 0 920806 56 2

ELIZABETH KOUHI *Round Trip Home*
    ISBN 0 920806 57 0

J. MICHAEL YATES *Insel: The Queen Charlotte Islands Meditations*
    ISBN 0 920806 58 9